Mother Goose in Sign

by S. Harold Collins

Illustrated by Kathy Kifer and Dahna Solar

Special thanks to the Larson Family
for their help and knowledge.

Published by
Garlic Press
100 Hillview Lane #2
Eugene, OR 97401

ISBN 0-931993-66-0
Order No. GP-066

Mother Goose In Sign presents traditional Mother Goose nursery rhymes fully illustrated in Signed English.

Enjoy not only the whole rhyme but realize that *One, Two, Buckle My Shoe* teaches numbers, *Solomon Grundy* teaches days of the week, and *Thirty Days Has September* teaches months.

Most vocabulary is standard Signed English, but there are some liberties with signs to accommodate the language of aged rhymes—stile (fence ladder), sixpence (six penny), gander (male goose).

- Solomon Grundy
- Thirty Days Has September
- One, Two, Buckle My Shoe
- Old Mother Goose
- The Crooked Sixpence

Solomon Grundy

Solomon Grundy,

born

on

Monday,

christened

on

Tuesday,

married

on

Wednesday,

became

ill

on

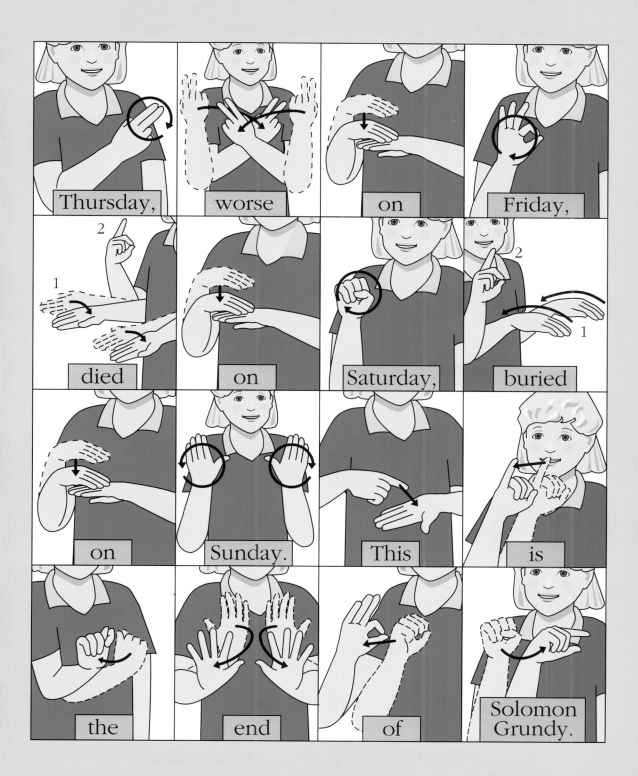

Thirty Days
Has September

Thirty	days	has	September,
April,	June,	and	November;
February	has	twenty-eight	alone,

All the rest have thirty-one, except leap-year, that is the time when February has twenty-nine.

One, Two, Buckle My Shoe

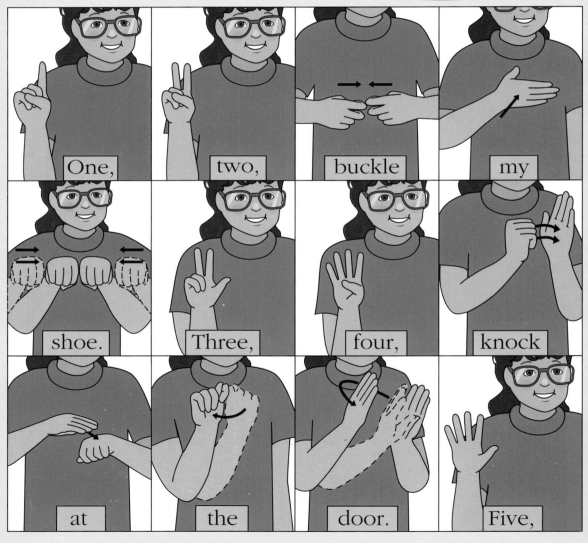

One, two, buckle my shoe. Three, four, knock at the door. Five,

Old Mother Goose

| Old | Mother | Goose, | when |

she wanted to wander,

would ride through the

air on a very

fine gander.

The Crooked Sixpence

There

was | a | crooked | man,

and | he | walked | a

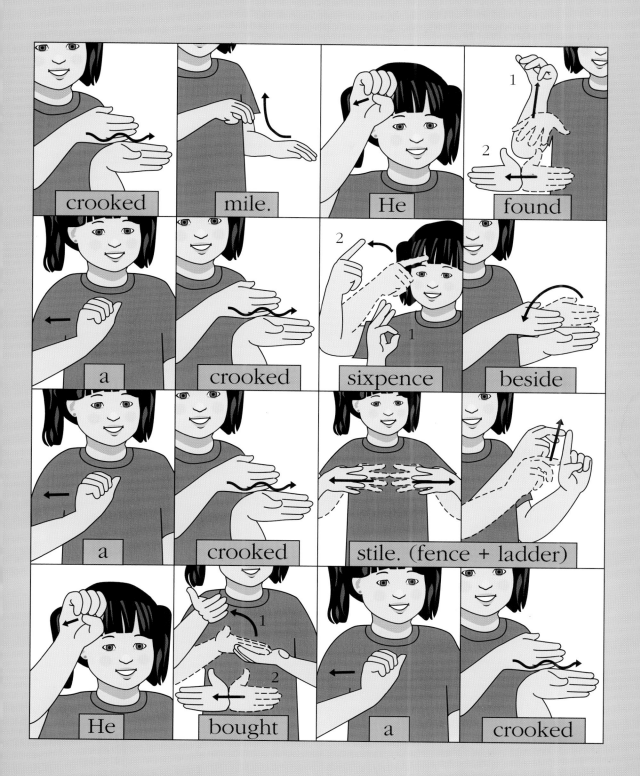